OBSIDIAN
A Glass Buttes Adventure

F. Scott Crawford

ISBN-10: 1-48120-452-1
ISBN-13: 978-1481204521

DEDICATION

For Maggie, "forever & forever."

A side-notched Desert Redding style arrow point, made by the author from transparent "Midnight Lace" obsidian from Glass Buttes, 2009 A.D.

Welcome To The "Glass Buttes" Volcanoes In Eastern Oregon.

From the 1990's until 2010, every summer in late June and again in late September a group of 10 to 12 students gathered for several days of obsidian knapping instruction, demonstrations and practice at Glass Buttes, in eastern Oregon.

This "flint knapping" Workshop was long hosted by Craig Ratzat as a teaching service to the customers of his www.Neolithics.com website, a source of knapping stone and tools for knappers of all ages and levels of expertise, from beginners to advanced.

Personally, I have been to four of Craig's Knapping Workshops over the last ten or twelve years. The Glass Buttes instructions and demonstrations have been instrumental in helping me advance along my journey through the wonders of stone tool making.

In addition, all of us students have been able to pick the brains of a number of alumni of the Workshops. These are previous students who have excelled in learning and mastering the knapping craft. They show up again and again to give support and encouragement to the new breakers of stone.

Plus, they all just love to razz the teacher ... and share stories about all the giant stones they dug out in the old days, when they had to work barefoot in the obsidian fields and quarry out the stone for class with their bare hands, etc., etc. Really, I think they just come around for the camp food!

I thought it would be interesting for rockhounds and students of native population technologies to bring you a glimpse of the seldom seen world of flint knapping (it is pretty much just obsidian knapping up here on Glass Buttes).

This activity has gone on for thousands of years, and has somehow remained a secret society, with very little public acknowledgement of its products, its teaching and its vast influence on all aspects of modern technology.

Some folks are absolutely sure that without the ground- and stone-breaking research performed by curious and hungry flint knappers through the untold millennia of human history, there would be no space age, no modern transportation systems, no iron and steel construction materials, no copper pennies or electrical wiring, and, of all things, no internet!

It is an absolute certainty that if ancient knappers had not been seeking out all the good sources of sharp and workable stone, we would never have mastered the natural resources which are so integral to modern life.

That's enough propaganda!

Now, let's take a behind-the-scenes look at what really happens when flint knappers of all levels of skill get together for a few days of exploration and "limited" exploitation of the incredible obsidian flows which have been known and utilized at Glass Buttes for thousands of years.

Come along through the next few pages, here at mile post 77, east of Bend, Oregon on Highway 20.

FSC

Quarrying Rock!

The first thing you learn at one of Craig Ratzat's Glass Buttes Workshops is that you cannot break rock until you have learned how to obtain it.

Out here on the slopes of this ancient volcano, that can mean digging into the old flows of obsidian mixed with pumice and ash.

And naturally, the larger pieces which you would like to obtain are deeply buried.

Sometimes a few minutes of overburden removal is all that is needed. But, sometimes that process can take hours of work ... in the hot, dry summer sunshine.

As you can see, there are also areas on the mountain where you can simply pick up nice size chunks of obsidian and place them in a bucket.

These are areas where the slow moving obsidian flow emerged from cracks in the surface and individual pieces tumbled down the hill side.

Supervising!

Another thing you soon discover is that the trenches for quarrying are not always very wide. Maybe one or two people can work side by side.

That means that the rest of your group gets to take a break while you are sweating away down in the rock pit.

They do have to learn how to supervise the labor of others. After all, how else will they see your special talent for making dirt fly.

All the time, you wonder what this has to do with knapping stone?

And then, that one great boulder of obsidian comes loose at your feet. Now it is yours!

A Few Good Chunks Of Obsidian ... 4 Days Of Knapping.

So, you roll that chunk of stone out of the pit. With every intention of setting it aside so that you and you alone can work on it.

Your head is full of visions of sunshine glinting on the freshly fashioned obsidian blades and points which you are going to produce.

And just let somebody else pick up your chunk! Ha!

Yet, in just a few more minutes of digging you roll out two or three more nice boulders of volcanic glass.

Pretty soon you have no idea which piece it was that you so treasured, and you just dig on through the stone, knowing that you will have all that you can break for the next week, after you and your fellow students have completed your quarrying activities.

"But It Looks So Easy!"

This side broke during the notching process of this Calf Creek style spearpoint. Just a little twist out of line with your hand or tool and you can split the blade lengthwise like this.

"99 Attaboys! = 1 Oh $*%@!"

Each teaching session involves discussion and demonstration of a different stage in the preparation of raw material for and then the actual production of knapped tools. Craig clearly shows the processes to the group and then works with each individual student to evaluate and refine their skills.

As he teaches and demonstrates the skilled results of many years of practice and careful thought about his work, new students and long-time friends alike loudly echo their respect for his expertise and their frustration at their own pace of knapping development across the mountain slopes: "We hate Craig Ratzat!"

Of course, that sentiment initially caused Craig some discomfort. But today, after considering the great respect in which his students hold him, Craig just grins and answers back:

"It's alright to hate Craig Ratzat!"

"Flute That Thing!"

One of Craig's early students regularly comes to the Glass Buttes workshops, bringing hope and inspiration to each new group of knapping enthusiasts.

Mike's favorite project is the production of Clovis style spearheads. With several years of dedicated practice, he has become very proficient in the hand fluting of these defining tools of the very earliest explorers of North America.

As he works, Craig's new students and Mike's long-time friends alike loudly encourage his signature objective: "Flute that thing!"

First On This Mountain?

Glass Buttes is one of those places where every step you take is likely to be exactly where another man, woman or child walked before you, sometimes as long as 12,000 years ago.

Their footprints may not be visible to you, but the protected evidence of their activities abounds.

Keep your eyes open and you might find a dart point hidden in the ground hugging leaves of the high mountain slopes. Maybe it was made by a youngster, who was learning to work the stone, just like you.

It is almost a sacred place; where the secrets of working this amazing volcanic stone have been passed down for over four hundred generations.

You Can See 12,000 Years!

Glass Buttes at sunset does incredible things to your vision. At the right time of year you can still see the native big game like elk, mule deer and antelope. And, when you squint your eyes in exactly the correct manner, looking out across the miles and back through the years, you can still see the ancient hunters stalking their prey across the valleys below the far mountain ridges of the Oregon desert.

A Natural Place To Sit, Work And Watch For Dinner.

Hundreds, even thousands, of years ago, native craftsmen would sit on this stone bench near the top of Glass Buttes.

From this elevated shelf of the mountain, they could see for many miles across the valleys and mountains.

As they sat to work on obsidian tools, they could also keep an eye out for herds to hunt tomorrow, or observe the progress of an active hunt below.

How do we know this?

Because some left their unfinished tools behind, here along a seldom seen natural stone wall high up on the mountain. Their preforms of obsidian remain to this day, hopefully undisturbed in this sacred home place forever.

Some would say that in the mountain wind you can still hear their quiet conversations as they sit at work.

If you sit near here and listen to your heart, it is indeed possible that you can still watch the long story of their lives unfold in the valley below you.

Night Falls With Brilliant Colors In Eastern Oregon's Desert Landscape.

You and I might have been born in the era of flight and the beginning of the Space Age, but often we find our hearts and souls yearning for a simpler time. For a time when survival itself was often a great accomplishment which depended on our own effort and skill.

One way this manifests in our lives is this interest and obsession with making stone tools and weapons just like our ancestors did all over the world, for thousands of all-too-often forgotten generations.

Maybe that's why we gotta break rock!

I say "Go for it!"

Learn to master this ancient craft and art which we call "Flint Knapping".

Then you too will enjoy your new-found ability to turn rock and stone into useful tools and hunting weapons.

Rebuild your link with the creative and resourceful human beings who have gone before us all.

That's why I wrote the correspondence course "FLINT KNAPPING 20.12" ... to help us all make the connection to our history and to our past.

Get on that "Fast Track" to learn the ancient and honorable art and craft of creating tools and hunting weapons out stone ... "Flint Knapping".

Subscribe today.

FLINT KNAPPING 20.12™

www.StoneBreaker-FSC.net/FLINT_KNAPPING_20-12.html

"Midnight Lace" Obsidian -- Knapped Of Stone From Glass Buttes in Eastern Oregon. Backlit To Demonstrate The Transparency Of This Volcanic Natural Glass.

Knapped From Glass Buttes Obsidian During The 2007 A.D. Workshop.

"Rainbow" ... "Mahogany" ... "Silver Sheen" ... "Gray Green KawKaw" ... "Midnight Lace" ... "Brown" ... "Tiger Stripe" ... some of the colorful varieties of volcanic obsidian found on the slopes and ridges of Glass Butte and Little Glass Butte in Lake County of eastern Oregon.

Here are four different styles of ancient tools and hunting weapons *(enlarged about 50%)* which were made by the author during the June 2007 "Glass

Buttes Workshop" hosted by Craig Ratzat, master flint knapper and proprietor of www.Neolithics.com ... the supply house for knapping tools and stone.

Those of us who enjoyed traveling to Glass Buttes, breaking chunks of obsidian into spalls and blades and learning to master the ancient craft of stone knapping from Craig and his oft-returning "Glass Buttes Workshop" alumni will always treasure the memories and skills which we learned on the dry and dusty slopes of these old volcanoes.

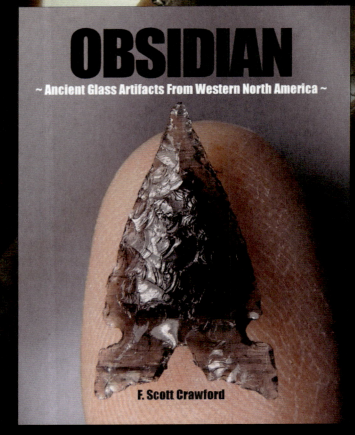

This Is Your Personal Invitation To Add This New Book To Your Artifacts Library. $149.95. Simply Click On The Direct Link To Amazon At The Bottom Of This Page:

OBSIDIAN
~ Ancient Glass Artifacts From Western North America

Perhaps a "Kennewick" lance point, 6-5/8" long, found 1940's - 1950's in northern California's Modoc County. Ex-Byron Anderson Collection. Paleo Period, 11,000 - 9000 B.P.

OBSIDIAN
~ Ancient Glass Artifacts From Western North America ~

F. Scott Crawford

www.Amazon.com/dp/1731489404

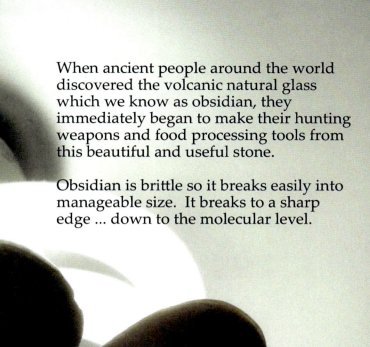

When ancient people around the world discovered the volcanic natural glass which we know as obsidian, they immediately began to make their hunting weapons and food processing tools from this beautiful and useful stone.

Obsidian is brittle so it breaks easily into manageable size. It breaks to a sharp edge ... down to the molecular level.

No man-made material provides a sharper edge. So, it cuts and slices, it shreds and dices.

Obsidian is tough enough to use as projectile points for hunting purposes. Whether on the business end of a hand-held lance or a throwing javelin or on the tip of a smaller throwing dart propelled powerfully by an *"atlatl"* or on the *"pointy end"* of a smaller stick or reed as an arrow shot from a bow.

*A 7/8" long **"Calapooya"** arrowhead, found in the early 1900's near Sodaville in Linn County, Oregon, by William Kirkland. It was in his family's artifact collection for over 100 years. Ex-Charles Blake for the William Kirkland Family Collection. Development to Historic Phase, 1000 - 200 B.P.*

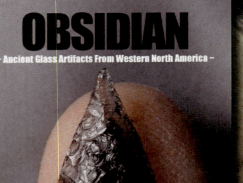

A 1-5/8" long, transparent, clear obsidian **"Elko Split Stem"** dart point or knife blade, found in the late 1800's - early 1900's in Humboldt County, northern Nevada, by William Kirkland. It was in his family's artifact collection for over 100 years. Ex-Charles Blake for the William Kirkland Family Collection. Late Archaic Period to Developmental Phase, 3500 - 1200 B.P.

Left and Right: A **"Snake River Dart"** point, 1-15/16" long, found at the **"OO Ranch"** in eastern Oregon's Harney County, in the 1940's. Ex-Byron Anderson Collection. Transitional to Classic Phase, 2000 - 700 B.P.

OBSIDIAN
~ Ancient Glass Artifacts From Western North America ~

Why Do I Make Arrowheads?
Can This Obsession & Passion Be Explained?

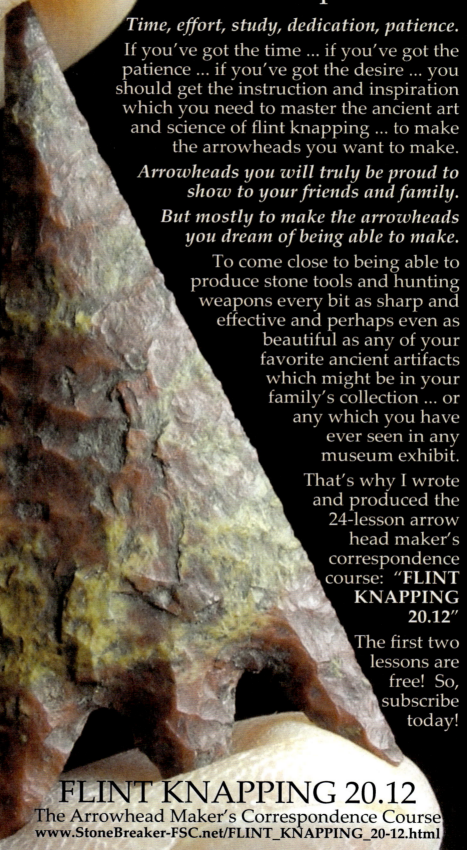

Why do I spend so much time and effort making and writing about making stone tools and hunting weapons?

Take a close look at this photograph.

It shows a 1,000 year old jasper arrowhead found in northern California over 40 years ago.

Artifacts like this are what drive me. I want to be able to make stone projectile points like this.

With the same methods and tools as those which were used by an ancient "flint knapper" so long ago.

And, you know what else?

This is just one of two matching arrow points which were found ... made from two different pieces of the same stone.

If you have the least bit of interest in learning how to make stone arrow heads, this will inspire you. It will challenge you ... it will drive you.

You know it's not easy.

You know it takes patience. You know it takes persistence. And you know it takes time.

Time, effort, study, dedication, patience.

If you've got the time ... if you've got the patience ... if you've got the desire ... you should get the instruction and inspiration which you need to master the ancient art and science of flint knapping ... to make the arrowheads you want to make.

Arrowheads you will truly be proud to show to your friends and family.

But mostly to make the arrowheads you dream of being able to make.

To come close to being able to produce stone tools and hunting weapons every bit as sharp and effective and perhaps even as beautiful as any of your favorite ancient artifacts which might be in your family's collection ... or any which you have ever seen in any museum exhibit.

That's why I wrote and produced the 24-lesson arrow head maker's correspondence course: **"FLINT KNAPPING 20.12"**

The first two lessons are free! So, subscribe today!

FLINT KNAPPING 20.12
The Arrowhead Maker's Correspondence Course
www.StoneBreaker-FSC.net/FLINT_KNAPPING_20-12.html

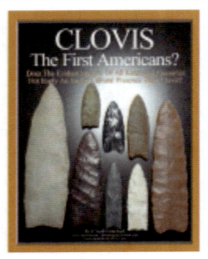

CLOVIS ~ The First Americans?
Does The Evident Mastery Of All Knapping Resources Not Imply An Earlier Cultural Presence Than Clovis?
ISBN-10: 1-47756-881-6
ISBN-13: 978-1477568811
$19.95

LITHICS ~ An American Heritage.
An Acquired Mastery Of The Natural Environment And Material Resources Is Clearly Demonstrated By High Quality Hunting Tools & Projectile Points
ISBN-10: 1-48108-075-X
ISBN-13: 978-1481080750
$14.95

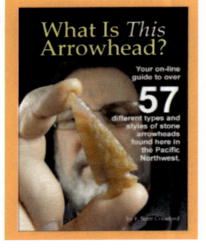

What Is *This* Arrowhead?
Your On-Line Guide To Over 57 Different Types And Styles Of Stone Arrowheads Found Here In The Pacific Northwest.
ISBN-10: 1-46637-853-0
ISBN-13: 978-1466378537
$34.95

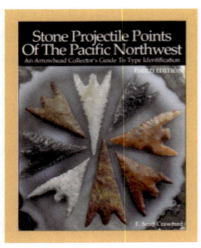

Stone Projectile Points Of The Pacific Northwest
An Arrowhead Collector's Guide To Type Identification
THIRD EDITION
ISBN-13: 979-8709395855
$59.95

Now You Can Get The Soft Cover Book Version Of
"OBSIDIAN ~ A Glass Buttes Adventure".
To Order On-Line, From Amazon.com, For Just $14.95,
Simply Click Right Now On The Following Secure Link:

https://www.Amazon.com/dp/1481204521

This 7" bifacial, bi-pointed stone blade was made by percussion and pressure flaking from a spall of "Rainbow" Obsidian from Glass Buttes in eastern Oregon. Produced by F. Scott Crawford in 2009 A.D., and photographed during a brief period of global cooling that occurred just after the winter solstice the following winter, on December 25, 2009.

AN "EARLY TO LATE ARCHAIC" STYLE ~ IS THIS THE LAST GREAT HUMBOLDT LANCE?

TRIPLE FLOW/MIDNIGHT LACE HUMBOLDT LANCE POINT.

An Early to Late Archaic style lance and dart point, or knife blade. Pressure flaked in 2008 A.D. by the author, by hand from a ground preform. Uniquely patterned, multi-colored and transparent obsidian from Glass Buttes: Triple Flow/Midnight Lace obsidian. 7-3/4" long by 1-3/4" wide. There is more information about this obsidian on the next page.

www.StoneBreaker-FSC.net

TRIPLE FLOW/MIDNIGHT LACE OBSIDIAN. Since the state of Oregon has slashed the amount of obsidian which can be collected at Glass Buttes by as much as 90%, as a practical matter, "Triple Flow/Midnight Lace" obsidian is no longer readily available except in those limited inventories of raw and cut stone now held in the personal stock of experienced flint knappers. In order to more efficiently make use of the limited quantity of this beautiful knapping stone, I have been using cut slabs, trimmed to general blade shape and ground to a convex cross section. These ground preform blades have been prepared by Craig Ratzat at www.Neolithics.com from his long-time inventory of Glass Buttes obsidian.

www.StoneBreaker-FSC.net

Black Knives Matter

10,000 years ago obsidian knives like this were used by the earliest people who explored North America. This technology contributed to the long term success of these pioneers at the end of the last Ice Age. And to all the cultures which inhabited North America over the thousands of years since that time. Explore the many styles of "Black Blades" which were used from the Paleo Period through the Archaic Period and up until recent times. You'll even see several modern made "Black Blades" made with the same ancient stone breaking techniques ... just so you will know that not all of the ancient survival skills of our ancestors are lost. Enjoy it all in the pages of "BLACK BLADES ~ For Those 'White Walkers' Of The Frozen North ~ ".

36 Stone Arrowheads For You To Make For Fun & Challenge

When you are learning to *"knap flint"* ... that is, to make arrowheads from stone as it has been done over the thousands of generations in human history ... the 36 different projectile points in the 106 page book, **"BREAK ROCK! Making Stone Arrowheads For Fun & Challenge"**, represent some of the finest examples of native American stone working craftsmanship and inventiveness. They are a worthy challenge. Making these arrowheads will give you that mystic connection, unlike any other, to the

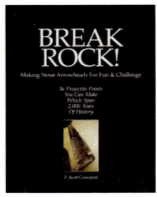

natural world which is so often missing in this age of computers and *"virtual reality"*. Let these ancient artifacts be the patterns you study. Let them be your guide to mastering a unique and challenging skill which you can enjoy for many years to come. Now, let's go break some rock!

BREAK ROCK!
Making Stone Arrowheads For Fun & Challenge

Click this link or go to:
www.Amazon.com/dp/1523393491

Made in the USA
Middletown, DE
11 December 2021

55214189R00020